AR 2.7
Pts. 0.5

NEB
X

FIRE SAFETY

Home
Fire Drills

by Lucia Raatma

Consultant:
Roy Marshall
State Fire Marshal of Iowa

Bridgestone Books
an imprint of Capstone Press
Mankato, Minnesota

Bridgestone Books are published by Capstone Press
818 North Willow Street, Mankato, Minnesota 56001
http://www.capstone-press.com

Library of Congress Cataloging-in-Publication Data
Raatma, Lucia.
    Home fire drills/by Lucia Raatma.
    p. cm.—(Fire safety)
    Includes bibliographical references and index.
    Summary: Explains the importance of planning what to do in case of fire in your
house and tells how practicing fire drills can help you to be safe.
    ISBN 0-7368-0195-2
    1. Fire drills—Juvenile literature. 2. Dwellings—Safety measures—Juvenile
literature. [1. Fire drills. 2. Dwellings—Safety measures. 3. Safety.] I. Title. II. Series:
Raatma, Lucia. Fire safety.
TH9445.D9R32 1999
628.9′22—dc21   98-47053
                                                                                            CIP
                                                                                            AC

Editorial Credits
Rebecca Glaser, editor; Timothy Halldin, cover designer; Kimberly Danger,
    photo researcher

Photo Credits
David F. Clobes, 6, 20
Gregg R. Andersen, cover, 8, 10, 12, 14, 16, 18
Unicorn Stock Photos/Martha McBride, 4

**Capstone Press would like to thank Nicholas Hermer, owner of Viking Fire and
Safety of Mankato, Minnesota, for providing equipment used in the photographs.**

Table of Contents

Fire Danger

Fires are dangerous if they get out of control. You must get out of your home fast during a fire. But you can stay safe if you plan ahead. Plan a fire escape route with your family. Practice fire drills at home.

Escape Routes

An escape route is a way to leave your home quickly and safely during a fire. Plan an escape route with your family. Draw a floor plan of your home that shows all doors and windows. Find at least two ways to exit each room. Choose a place to meet outside.

floor plan

a drawing that shows all the rooms, doors, and windows in your home

Doors as Exits

The main exit from each room is a door. But fire and smoke might be on the other side of a door. Touch the door quickly before you open it. Open the door only if it is cool. Keep the door closed if it is hot. Leave through a different exit if the door is hot.

Windows as Exits

A window is another way to exit a room. Plan your escape from high windows carefully. You may need to use an escape ladder. Ask an adult to show you how to use an escape ladder. Use an escape ladder only in an emergency.

emergency

a sudden danger; a home fire is an emergency.

Crawl Low

Smoke or fire sometimes can block all exits from a room. Smoke makes it hard to breathe. But air near the floor is clearer because smoke rises. You should stay low under the smoke. Crawl on your hands and knees to get outside.

Apartment Buildings

Use the stairs during a fire in an apartment building. Never use an elevator. Elevators can break during a fire. Stay in your apartment if your fire escape is blocked. Call the fire department to report where you are. Stay near a window and wave for help.

Meeting Place

Choose a meeting place as part of your escape route. Your family should meet at this place after they escape. The place could be a tree or mailbox. Call for help from a neighbor's home. Never go back into your home during a fire.

Smoke Alarms

Smoke alarms make a loud sound when they sense smoke. Your home should have at least one smoke alarm on each level. Adults should test smoke alarms once each month. Know what the smoke alarm sounds like. Be ready to escape if you hear the alarm.

Practice

Practice a home fire drill with your family twice each year. An adult should sound the smoke alarm. Each person should leave by a different exit on the escape route. Gather outside at your meeting place. Your family can stay safe if everyone is prepared.

Hands On: Surprise Fire Drill

It is important to get out of your home quickly during a fire. Practice your escape route to see how fast you can get outside. Practice your fire drill two times or more each year. Practice leaving from different rooms in your home.

<u>What You Need</u>

Smoke alarm

Escape route plan

An adult to help

Two or more family members

Stopwatch

<u>What You Do</u>

1. Have an adult sound the smoke alarm without telling you. The drill should be a surprise.
2. An adult should use the stopwatch to time each drill.
3. Go outside when you hear the alarm. Follow your escape route plan. Use the exit nearest to you.
4. Have an adult block certain exits so you can practice using other exits.
5. Meet your family outside at your planned meeting place.
6. The adult will tell you how long it took.

Words to Know

escape route (ess-KAPE ROOT)—a planned way to leave your home; escape routes should have two ways to leave each room and a place outside to meet your family.

exit (EG-zit)—a way out of a building

prepared (pree-PAIRD)—knowing what to do ahead of time

prevent (pree-VENT)—to stop something before it starts

smoke alarm (SMOHK uh-LARM)—a machine that senses smoke and warns people by making a loud sound

To Learn More

Loewen, Nancy. *Fire Safety.* Plymouth, Minn.: Child's World, 1997.

Raatma, Lucia. *Safety around Fire.* Safety First! Mankato, Minn.: Bridgestone Books, 1999.

Internet Sites

Fire Prevention for Kids
http://www.prairienet.org/~xx010/FirePreventionForKids1.html
Sparky's Home Page
http://www.sparky.org/
U.S. Fire Administration (USFA) Kids Homepage
http://www.usfa.fema.gov/kids/

Index